Table of Contents

* *

Table of Contents, Continued

IX (Nine) By Gwen

A Collection of Poetry and Reflection

ISBN# 978-0-578-85438-0

Written, Edited, and Published
By Gwen Woodson

I can do all things through Christ who strengthens me.

Philippians 4:13

Poem 1

The Skin I'm In

By: Gwen Woodson

The Skin I'm In Does Not Wrinkle or Crack, My Cocoa Butter Lining Keeps It All in Tact;

The Skin I'm In Is Sweet like Honey, Chocolate like Cake, Smooth like Carmel, Hydrated like a Great Lake;

The Skin I'm In Does Not Stumble or fall; because I am Forced Daily to Keep Standing Tall;

The Skin I'm In Is the Silk of All Fabric, Delicate like a Butterfly, Has Absolutely No Static;

The Skin I'm In Simmers like a Coffee Bean, So Do I Shed It Because the World Is So Mean;

I Must Embrace This Skin, I Need to Love Myself, If Not For That, How Could I Love Anybody Else;

The Skin I'm in is My Melanin, That Melts like Hot Chocolate with Marshmallows in My Cup;

Of Course I Have No Intentions of Giving That All Up;

The Skin I'm In Keeps My Hips Round, My Lips Plump and Bright; The Thick of My Thighs; The Light in My Almond Shaped Eyes;

The Skin I'm In Keeps My Hair Frizzy and Busy; Needing to Be Tamed like the Lion Roaring Inside;

The Skin I'm in is soft like Butter; You Know They Say I Got It from My Mother;
The Skin I'm In Runs Deep Within; it's My Badge of Honor, I Can Not Pretend;

The Skin I'm In Is Controversial, but I Must Wear It, I'm Not a Commercial, But an Authentic Masterpiece of Gods Devine Plan;

It's the Legacy of Being Brown, You Know like Chocolate Chip Rounds, Rich like Fudge, This Was No Mistake, I Was Fine Tuned in the Oven Till My Shade Was Done;

This Skin I'm In Is Right Not Wrong; I Will Wear the Skin I'm In until God Calls Me Home

Reflection 1

She was poetry, but he could not read. She Was Poetry, but He Could Not Understand.

Inspiration One

"The Skin I'm In" Was Inspired by an Epiphany.

After Years of Struggling with Self Love, Self-Encouragement, Self-Motivation, Self-Empowerment; I decided to let go, and let God teach me to Love Myself as whole, for who I am, what I am. I then studied myself for weeks, and started to write down the things I loved about me the most. From there I saw that I am Beautiful, I am a Masterpiece, I am Gods Chosen, I am Powerful within myself, and the Skin I'm in is Enough...

I am Enough.

Gwen Woodson

Poem 2

From The Cotton Fields to the Kingdom

By: Gwen Woodson

The longest days, the heat of the sun rays; burning through me like a furnace; as I pick until my fingers bleed; fall to my knees from a tired spell; but no one to tell; that the cotton field, is not my home;

I feel alone, as I look to the skies; with tears in my eyes, asking God for a sign; that my days and time, in the fields of no one's dreams; will come to a sudden end;

The time seems to stop; as the sweat drops; down my entire being; so much cotton to collect; no respect for a slave; will be worked to the grave; unless my super natural steps in and begins, to take me from the cotton fields to the kingdom;

I was told I was a Queen; my palace awaits; behind some pearly gates, I've never seen;

Years go by, as my children, join me under the blue sky; we become a field full of work horses;

The crisp on our bodies, from the blazing sun, starts to shine; every time; the fields fill with fluffy white substance; that becomes our daily bread; no shed in sight for a break during the day; waiting on the night; to fall so the sun can rest and so can I;

From time to time, I daydream about one day, when the cotton fields are just a memory of my sweltering labor; no more I say; but every day this is the place, I must be;

I wonder, is the real me buried somewhere on an island of cotton, or does my freedom await;

The field is not always kind to us all; some fall, never to arise again; so we gather and we pray; that someday, we will be free;

One evening as the sun went down; I walked around the fluffy cotton field; blooming time; so beautiful to be around;

I then heard an unfamiliar sound; it was a voice of reason;

He said it's your season; to break every chain; I listened as I walked slowly towards my destiny;

I felt my crown sit atop my head; as I walked a long way home; Layed down in my bed and dreamed;

When the sun rose again, my eyes opened wide; I realized my King left a message that said;

Here are the keys you prayed for; the keys you stayed for; a new fresh place awaits;

No more pain, or shame, or blistered limbs;

Time to live, create new memories; your palace has been prepared;

You made it; from the Cotton Fields to the Kingdom

Reflection 2

Sometimes you have to Live the Lie, In Order to Find Your Truth.

Inspiration Two

"From the Cotton Fields to The Kingdom" was inspired by a Canvas Painting I saw one day while going through my news feed on Facebook.

The image was of a Beautiful Black Woman, walking through a blooming cotton field, as she walked, she was putting a crown up on her head with one hand, and dropping the chains from her wrist with the other hand.

It was a breathtaking image. I knew at that moment, I would write about her... I knew at that moment the Piece I wrote would be called

"From the Cotton Fields to the Kingdom"

Gwen Woodson

Poem 3

I Will Wear My Crown

By: Gwen Woodson

I am a Queen, I Will Wear My Crown; the Worlds Negativity Can't Weigh Me Down;

I come from a Blood Line of Majesty; My Father King Jesus gave my crown to me

My Riches don't come from Wealth or Money; My Faith is my Millionaire Fruit;

He Keeps It Coming

My Crown Sparkles In the Day; It Sparkles In the Night;

Perfectly Fit, Radiates My Light

When I look in the Mirror What Do I see;

Courage, Beauty, Strength, the Spirit in Me

I wear my Crown Proudly; Accept My Queen Status Loudly;

Man Can Not Comprehend the Jewels and grander of my Crown; My Net Worth Is My Faith, My Joy, My Peace, My Hope, My Daily Turn Around

Calling Myself a Queen Sounds Like a Cliché; I Will Wear My Crown, No One Can Take That Away; I Know For Certain It Is Here To Stay;

I come from a Blood Line of Majesty; My Father King Jesus gave my crown to me

Reflection 3

Diamonds are Rare, and so are you.

Inspiration Three

"I Will Wear My Crown" was Inspired by the realization that I am the Daughter of a King. I am a Beautiful, Strong, Amazing, and Talented Black Queen.

For The Rest of my Life, every day I wake and rise,

"I Will Wear My Crown"

Gwen Woodson

Poem 4

TODAY

BY: GWEN WOODSON

AS I RISE WITH THE MORNING SUN, THE LIGHT OF THE DAY COMES IN, AND I KNOW ITS TIME TO BEGIN A NEW ADVENTURE CALLED TODAY;

THE LIGHT SOUND OF THE WIND AND THE SINGING BIRDS LETS ME KNOW I'M IN TUNE WITH NATURES BEAUTY, AND SO I'M ALL IN FOR AN OPPORTUNITY CALLED TODAY;

MY HEART BEATS TO THE SOUND OF MY TICKING CLOCK, AS IT GOES OFF WITH THAT SONG I CHOSE AND I KNOW IT MEANS THERE IS A FRESH TODAY;

MY EARS RING TO THIS THING CALLED NOISE AND I KNOW THAT I HAVE THE ABILITY TO HEAR WHAT AND WHO IS SPEAKING TO ME TODAY;

I MARVEL AT THE REST I RECEIVED FROM THE LONG WEEKS END; SO I STRETCH TO THE HEAVENS, I PRAY AND I THANK GOD AGAIN FOR TODAY

Reflection 4

Every day is a new chance, choice and opportunity, To Get It Right.

Inspiration Four

"Today" was inspired by waking up every day with a Grateful heart and being Thankful; not for any one particular thing, but for everything.

Make "Today" count each time you are graced with another chance at Life.

Gwen Woodson

Poem 5

SPREADING MY WINGS

By: Gwen Woodson

MY WINGS HAVE GROWN, I FEEL SO STRONG, IM FLYING HIGH IM NOT ALONE;

IM COVERED IN THE BLOOD BECAUSE IT'S BETTER THAN THE MUD;

MY FAITH PUSHES ME; GOOD SPIRITS KEEP MOVING ME;

 TO A LEVEL OF EXCELLENCE THAT ONLY GOD CAN SEE;

THE ROAD IS LONG, BUT MY WINGS ARE STRONG, IM FLYING HIGH WHERE I BELONG;

MY PEACE KEEPS ME, CONSTANTLY;

ANGELS SURROUND ME;

MY WINGS HAVE GROWN, I FEEL SO STRONG, IM FLYING HIGH IM NOT ALONE

Reflection 5

She flies not with the wind, but with the Angels.

Inspiration Five

"Spreading My Wings" Was inspired by Growth....

I am learning and growing in wisdom daily; And like the bird and the butterfly... I will spread my wings daily.

Gwen Woodson

Poem 6

Pretty Black

By: Gwen Woodson

I look in the mirror my reflection talks to me; the echo in my mind asks what you see;

I study my features, I throw my head back, I snap my fingers, I smile so big, because I'm simply Pretty Black;

My Chocolate Exterior is seen as a mediocre Accessory; it goes deeper than that; my melanin is like black gold, running through my veins; like an oil well full of that valuable thing, that only my pretty black can bring;

They Say I'm Not Good Enough, Light Enough, Thin Enough or Strong Enough;

I just step back and say, what you know about that Pretty Black;

Some Say I'm Angry; always on the attack; let's go to school, and learn the Truth about that Pretty Black;

Historical, Emotional, Lovable, Undeniable; The Mothers of Africa; Wrinkles and Shrivels Not;

Full of Soul, Spirituality, Nature's Bounty of Civility; Softer than Charmin, More Tender than a pot roast, just like that butter you spread on your toast;

The Coils in my Hair is the Crown that I share, with so many that look like me;

The Carriers of Great Pain; Has Shed More Tears than a hard Rain; Knocked Down to The Ground, but Keeps Getting Up Because that Pretty Black is More Sound than an Amplified Stadium of a Roaring Crowd;

Powerful in my Color, oh yes that's a Fact, I am unashamed to Say I'm Just Pretty Black

Reflection 6

My shade is my winning spade.

Inspiration Six

"Pretty Black"

The inspiration for this piece is very personal. It came from a colorism issue and conversation that one of my best friends and I often had.

She shared with me different experiences of her childhood, young adulthood, and her life in general. After meditating a many days on her trials, and her inner feelings, I wrote pretty black for her... She Is Beautiful Inside and Out. She Is "Pretty Black"

Gwen Woodson

Poem 7

It Was Just a Dream

By: Gwen Woodson

He had a Dream, that there would be no more nightmares;

Someone would open a door, and then care;

That my fingers would work to the bone, for a home, In America;

I heard she was this magical place; with lots of space, to hold all my wants and needs;

The food is plentiful, even though there is so much waste;

People there, do they care; or wade all day in their shallow pool;

While the kids go to school, and try to fit in;

If they don't, they just pretend to have friends; so no one knows they are lonely souls;

Why is this America, the place where dreams come true, where money is King;

Relevance is Material things;

No one sees the sadness, in their eyes;

Do they realize that hope is still alive and well; or do so many just dwell in their own minds;

Do you still find, that white picket fence, clothes on line; children in the sand box playing;

Dinner on time; a bedtime story, of sleeping tight after saying your prayers, and a healthy goodnight;

Are all the days gloomy; or is there still sunshine; like that soap opera says, just take one day at a time;

Is America the Beautiful; Yes it would seem, will we find our way;

Or is it all just a dream

Reflection 7
Dream Big, Dream Loud and Dream Often.

"It Was Just a Dream" Inspired by my outlook on the American Dream, in the eyes of family, friends, and the most Famous Dream of All, the one spoken about by the unforgettable Dr. Martin Luther King.

We all have a Dream; and someday, we will see those Dreams come True.

Gwen Woodson

Thank You For The Rain
By: Gwen Woodson

Lord Thank You For The Seeds, Thank You For The Growth, Thank You For The Flowers, Thank
You For The Trees;

I See The Birds Flying Free; Never Needing a Resource, As You Provide;

Their Wings Carry Them Through The Skies;

To Parks, Over The Airwaves, Over The Seas;

Just as Your Angel's Always Carry Me;

Thank You For The Butterflies, The Grasshopper and The Bees;

I Admire Your Storms, That Wash Away Clutter;
But Never My Dreams;

I'm In Awe With The Fresh Air, I Wake Up and Breathe;
After The Rain, There Is Nothing Better;
Rain Is Forever;

Everything Washed Clean;

Thank You For Pretty Green Grass, Flowers In Bloom;

Only The Rain Can Keep Them Growing; Just As You Keep Me Going;

Thank You For Laughter, For Love, and For Tears;

Thank You Lord For The Storms Of Life;
The Hurt, The Struggles, The Heartaches, The Pain;

Thank You Lord For Giving Us The Rain

Reflection 8

When life gives you lemons, make lemonade, and if you are still not Refreshed....

ADD ICE, and a SMILE

"Thank You for the Rain"

Inspired by my unwavering belief that the Lord provides us the Rain, and the Storms, to wash away all things that no longer need to be in our mist; allowing us to plant fresh seeds and harvest, in addition, allowing all things to grow and flourish into its new beginning and absolute potential.

Gwen Woodson

Poem 9

Victorious

By: Gwen Woodson

Victory Is Her Name, Loving God Is Her Game, She Has a Past, But Not Ashamed to Shout She's Victorious;

A Warrior, a Conquer, A Fighter; When She's Weighed Down, She Prays, and Then Feels Much Lighter;

She's Dedicated, Motivated, The Journey Is Long; He's Always There, He Keeps Her Strong;

She Shares Her Life with the Name Above All Names; She Keeps Him Close, He Knows Her Pain;

He Comforts, He Calms, He Counsels, He Reigns; Grace and Mercy, She Has Obtained;

Ask Someone about Him, They Will Tell You the Same;

She's Been Thru Fire, But Her Mind Is Clear and Oh So Sound;

There Is Victory in Her Smile, Her Walk, Her Talk, Her Life Turned Around;

She's Victorious

Reflection 9

God's gifts will make room for you, Keep Believing.

Inspiration Nine

"Victorious"

Because I am a Fighter, I am a Survivor; I am Strong,

I am Victorious!

Gwen Woodson

My Motto

"I don't write a poem and name it; I pick a title and then I claim it"

Gwen Woodson

Thank God for Every Blessing He has bestowed upon me.

Thank You To all my Family and Amazing Friends for your support and Love.

Today Only Comes once; Make it Count

About The Author

Gwen Woodson dreamed of being a published author since the young age of ten. Writing Poetry, through the joy and pain of real life experiences; never missing an opportunity to put her pen to paper, create and execute a poetic nature. Writing became a way of expressing what an often shy and quiet person could say out loud. Moving forward, she has a strong desire to expand her poetry library into several book collections of timeless reading for her family, friends, and a broader mainstream audience. Always keeping God First, true to self, and striving for excellence in all areas of her life; she knows that not giving up, staying strong and positive are absolutely necessary.

Special Acknowledgements

** To My Mother, Barbara Hodges-Woodson; and My Grandmother Joyce Hodges; because of your example, I know how to stand on my feet, always knowing that there is no such thing as too much prayer, compassion, patience, or love.

** To my close knit Tribe of nearest and dearest;

Thank You for always keeping our friendship genuine and real. Your unwavering support will never be forgotten.

**Amanda Torres-Tiffany

Thank You for all the beautiful imagery; for giving your time, and your talent to help me complete this journey.

I will always have a humble and sincere gratitude for your generosity.

Made in the USA
Las Vegas, NV
26 April 2021